CW00521311

REFLECTIONS OF LIFE'S JOURNEY

MONICA THOMPSON

For information on publishing, contact Journal Joy at Info@thejournaljoy.com.

www.thejournaljoy.com

Summary: In Reflections of Life's Journey, Monica Thompson embarks on a journey of self-reflection and worldwide observation. She ponders the world as we know it today in the midst of a global pandemic, as well as the AmeriKKKa our ancestors experienced in centuries both recent and long past. Her rawest emotions and experiences are transmuted into poetry as she writes about her familial relationships, her penned path ultimately leading her home—within, back to herself.

Paperback ISBN: 978-1-95775102-3

Hardcover ISBN: 978-1-957751-05-4

Edited by: Nicole Evans & Riel Felice

Author Website: www.monicathompson.biz

First paperback edition, 2022

JOURNAL JOY

An *Imprint* of Journal Joy *Publishers*

www.thejournaljoy.com

Dedication

I WOULD LIKE TO GIVE A HUGE THANK YOU TO MY BEAUTIFUL DAUGHTER, ASHLEIGH, FOR BEING MY STRENGTH AND SAVING ME.

THANK YOU, BABE, MY SPECIAL FRIEND, FOR ALWAYS AND FOREVER.

A SPECIAL THANKS TO MY MAGNIFICENT 7 FAMILY FOR ALWAYS BEING THERE (BARRY, DARRYL, STEPHANIE, SOPHIA, EDRI, SHARON, AND GUS).

SHOUT-OUT TO THE GRAYSONS—SHARNEE, DEE, RAYJON, DJ, AND DASJA—MY EXTENDED FAMILY.

THE THOMPSON CLAN, MY NIECES AND NEPHEWS, AND ALL THOSE WHO HAVE BEEN THERE FOR ME THROUGHOUT MY LIFE AND THIS JOURNEY.

I THANK GOD DAILY FOR MY TALENTS, MY STRENGTH, AND ALL MY BLESSINGS.

CONTINUE RESTING IN HEAVENLY PEACE, CLAUDIO. WITHOUT YOU, THIS PASSION WOULD HAVE NEVER MANIFESTED. RICHIE BERMUDEZ, MY BEST FRIEND; AND MY DAD, ALFONSO FERDINAND GOODWIN, WHO INSPIRED ME TO BE A STRONG, INDEPENDENT WOMAN.

CONTENTS

A LETTER TO MY DEAR SON

My Dear Son, Claudio,

I love you more than you knew; you were my angel all the while. From birth! knew you were blessed with amazing talents. Your fearlessness and zest for life always inspired me. You knew what you wanted and didn't let anything stop you from achieving your goals. Your spirit shined so brightly and affected all who crossed your path. The bond that our family shared was more than that between mother, brother, and sister; it was a tightly woven understanding of unconditional love and trust for one another. We laughed together; we cried together; we lived for one another.

I was the one who was truly blessed on April 7, 1986, and when the doctor said, "Congratulations! *It's a boy,*" I was overwhelmed with joy. Little did I know that on June 19, 2014, God had a bigger and better plan for you. You were my angel for 28 years, and now, it's time for you to watch over other people and touch their lives as you have mine. And, although you are not here with me, I shall always embrace and cherish the time I shared with you.

Claudio, you brought such joy, comfort, and peace to my life! I love you, CJ. I love you and miss you, Claudio Gene Lake, aka Maddox Madison. You're forever in my heart.

From your SuperWoman, as you would say.

Mommy

EIGHT YEARS

I CAN'T BELIEVE IT'S BEEN EIGHT YEARS
I STILL CRY THOSE SAME TEARS
WISHING YOU WERE STILL HERE

IF I HAD ONE WISH IT WOULD BE
THAT YOU COULD COME BACK TO ME
AND BE WITH ME ETERNALLY

YOU WERE MY AMAZING SON
GOD'S CHOSEN ONE
YOUR LIFE HAD JUST BEGUN

SOMETIMES I QUESTION WHY
HE CHOSE YOU TO DIE
GOD GAVE YOU YOUR WINGS SO YOU COULD
SOAR AND FLY HIGH

ONE DAY WE'LL MEET AGAIN
IN GOD'S HOUSE, OUR HEAVEN
I'LL KEEP YOUR MEMORY ALIVE, MADDOX
MADISON

GOOD NIGHT MY TURTLE DOVE
MY PROTECTION FROM ABOVE
MY FIRST TRUE LOVE

CONTINUE SLEEPING WITH THE ANGELS
CLAUDIO GENE LAKE
A/K/A MADDOX MADISON 4/7/86 - 6/19/14

JUNETEENTH

ON JUNE 19, 1865
WAS THE DAY SLAVERY SHOULD HAVE DIED.
THEY WERE TOLD WE WERE FREE
TWO AND A HALF YEARS AFTER THE SURRENDER BY
GENERAL ROBERT E. LEE.
THE EMANCIPATION PROCLAMATION WAS
ORIGINALLY SIGNED ON JANUARY 1, 1983. THIS WAS
A CHANGE IN HIS STORY, OR HISTORY.

ON JUNETEENTH,
IN THE YEAR OF 2014
AN ANGEL CAME TO ME
I MUST TAKE YOUR SON
HE IS THE CHOSEN ONE.
AS HE WENT UP INTO THE LIGHT
A NEW STAR BEGAN SHINING BRIGHT

THIS DAY WILL ALWAYS HAVE MIXED EMOTIONS
FOR ME.
DO I CELEBRATE OUR "FREEDOM,"?
ESPECIALLY WHEN WE ARE STILL EXPERIENCING
HATE AND PREJUDICE FROM SOME?
OR DO I CONTINUE REMEMBERING THIS DAY AS
THE DAY MY SON WAS TAKEN AWAY?

I WILL HAVE SOME GOOD TIMES THIS DAY.

I WILL ALSO TAKE TIME TO PRAY.
HOPING AND PRAYING THAT ONE DAY,
THE WORDS OF MLKING WILL COME TO PASS:
FREE AT LAST; FREE AT LAST.

BEGINNINGS

IT ALL BEGAN THE DAY YOUR
LIFE ENDED.

I BEGAN WRITING TO KEEP SANE. THOUGHT
WRITING COULD EASE MY PAIN.

EVERY DAY, I THINK OF YOU, GRIEVING THE THINGS
WE CAN NO LONGER DO.

I MISS YOU SO MUCH: YOUR LAUGHTER,
YOUR TENDER TOUCH.

WE WERE LIKE ONE,
MY LOVE, MY SON.

EVERY DAY SEEMS SO LONG. YOUR SISTER,
ASHLEIGH, HELP KEEPS ME STRONG.

I PRAY TO GOD EVERY NIGHT
TO HELP ME FIND MY LIGHT.

LORD, MY LIFE SEEMS SO DIM.
I'M TRULY MISSING HIM.

I HAVE MANY SLEEPLESS NIGHTS.
LORD, HELP ME SHINE SO BRIGHT.

I'M TIRED OF THESE DARK DAYS. IS
MY GRIEF HERE TO STAY?

I'LL KEEP MOVING ON. I'LL KEEP
TRYING TO BE STRONG

UNTIL WE MEET AGAIN IN
HEAVEN.

MY BEAUTIFUL GIRL

I HAVE A SPECIAL LOVE FOR A GIRL.
SHE IS MY ENTIRE WORLD.

I WILL FIGHT AND EVEN SLAUGHTER
FOR SHE IS MY BEAUTIFUL DAUGHTER.

WHEN SHE SPITS HER RHYMES, IT'S A-BLAZIN'.
SHE'S KNOWN AROUND THE WORLD AS "AMAZIN."

THE LOVE I HAVE FOR HER LIFE,
IS THE LOVE SHE HAS FOR HER FUTURE WIFE.

WHAT I HAVE NOW WILL ONE DAY BE YOURS.
YOU DESERVE HEALTH, WEALTH, AND SO MUCH
MORE.

WE'VE BEEN THROUGH SOME GOOD TIMES, BAD
TIMES, AND NIGHTMARES.
BABY GIRL, KNOW I'LL ALWAYS BE THERE.

YOU'VE GROWN INTO A BEAUTIFUL YOUNG LADY.
YOU'RE ENGAGED; WILL BE MARRIED AND HAVE A
BABY.

I'M SO PROUD OF WHO YOU'VE BECOME.
SO THANKFUL TO YOU, MY CHOSEN ONE.

OUR BOY IS SO PROUD OF WHAT YOU HAVE DONE
YOUR BIG BROTHER, MY BELOVED SON.

SO, CONTINUE LIVING YOUR BEST LIFE.
BUILD A FUTURE NOW FOR YOU AND YOUR
FUTURE WIFE.

CONTINUE DOING YOUR ABSOLUTE BEST.
NEVER SETTLE FOR ANYTHING LESS.

A NAME THAT ONE DAY WILL BE GREAT
LISTEN OUT FOR ASHLEIGH DOMONIQUE LAKE.

MY FATHER

YOU WALKED WITH THOSE VERY LONG STRIDES. I WATCHED YOU WITH AMAZING PROUD EYES.

I GREW UP WITHOUT A DAD TO HUG ME. NOW, I'M YOUR DAUGHTER, AND YOU'RE MY FAMILY.

MY MOM WAS MARRIED ONE, TWO, AND THREE, BUT YOU WERE THE BEST FATHER FOR ME.

YOU HAD YOUR OWN DAUGHTERS, DONNA, SHEILA, JOYCE, AND DEE. NOW, YOU HAVE MY BROTHER QUE AND ME.

MY LIFE BECAME GREAT WHEN WE BECAME A FAMILY OF EIGHT.

REMEMBERING THE COOKOUTS, VACATIONS, AND MEMORIES WE HAD; DAMN, I MISS MY FRIEND, MY MENTOR, MY BEST DAD.

I MIMICKED MY LIFE AFTER YOU FROM SPORTS, BOOKS, AND THE SAME JOB, TOO.

GOD SAW FIT TO GIVE YOU YOUR WINGS. HE KNEW YOU HAD DONE SO MANY AMAZING THINGS.

THANK YOU FOR BEING AN AMAZING DAD; THE BEST DAD A GIRL COULD EVER HAVE.

I HAVE SO MUCH MORE TO SAY. I DEDICATED THIS
POEM TO YOU. HAPPY BIRTHDAY.

Alfonso Ferdinand Goodwin 1/7/39-1/21/2012

THE ENDING

NOT A DAY GOES BY
THAT I DON'T CRY.
ASKING MYSELF WHY
YOU HAD TO DIE.

I FEEL SAD
SOMETIMES, EVEN MAD,
REMEMBERING WHAT WE HAD,
MISSING MY SON AND MY DAD.

HOW COULD THIS BE
THAT YOU HAD TO LEAVE ME?
I'M STILL IN DISBELIEF—
OR IS IT JUST MY GRIEF?

NOW, I'M ALL ALONE.
I CAN'T CALL YOU ON THE PHONE.
JUST SITTING HERE AT HOME;
WRITING THIS LONELY POEM.

I PRAY YOU'RE DOING WELL
WHILE I LIVE HERE IN HELL
FEELS LIKE I'M UNDER A SPELL
LISTENING FOR YOUR ANGEL'S BELL.

WHEN LIFE ENDS,

HOW DO YOU MEND?
I RECOMMEND
JUST PRAY. GOD, BLESS ME. AMEN.

GOOD MORNING SUNSHINE

Good morning, Sunshine! You're always on my mind. I hope you can see that you mean the world to me.

I could pray for fame and wealth, but all I pray for is your good health.

As time passes by, what you're going through may make you cry, but know I'll always be by your side.

Your healing process may seem long, but God's got you; He'll make you strong. Believe in Him and you'll never go wrong.

I'll always pray for healthier days. Your best of health means more than words can say.

Feel better soon. Love you from here to the moon!

Written for my Sis, Edri Roberts

RIP SUNFLOWER

As the days of July arrive, there come days with tears in your eyes.

The hurt never goes away, especially on that saddening day.

JAMELAH, your beautiful Sunflower, arose with God's power.

We miss her squeaky voice. When we think of her, our hearts rejoice.

JAMELAH is an angel above who is missed and truly LOVED.

Your mom is my guiding light. When I'm weak, she lets me know I'll be alright.

When my days and nights are long—**sometimes, I'm stuck and can't move on**—I think of the words of Edri telling me, *Mo*, stay strong.

Sleep in Heavenly Peace, Sunflower.
Continue to Protect us with God's power.

MAGIC SEVEN

POWER RANGERS IS WHERE WE BEGIN.
NOW, WE ARE THE MAGNIFICENT SEVEN.
I BELIEVE OUR GROUP WAS SENT FROM HEAVEN.

WE HAVE SEVEN DIFFERENT PERSONALITIES,
BUT Y'ALL ARE MY REALITY.
Y'ALL HELP KEEP ME GROUNDED, ACTUALLY.
Y'ALL ARE MY REAL FAMILY.
A GOD'S BLESSING, TRULY.

WE ARE FAMILY.
ALTHOUGH OUR ROOTS ARE FROM A DIFFERENT TREE,
OUR LOVE AND BOND EXIST UNCONDITIONALLY.

I LOVE YOU, SIX.
NEVER KNEW A LOVE LIKE THIS.
OUR BOND WILL ALWAYS EXIST.
OUR LOVE WILL NEVER BE DISMISSED.
IT WILL ALWAYS BE A BLISS.

WE HAVE A LOVE LIKE NO OTHER.
THAT'S WHY Y'ALL ARE MY SISTERS AND BROTHERS,
AND WE WILL ALWAYS HAVE LOVE FOR ONE ANOTHER.

YOU'LL BE MISSED

I HAVEN'T SEEN YOU IN A WHILE.

I SURE DID MISS YOUR SMILE
SHINING BRIGHTLY FOR MILES.

I STILL WONDER TODAY WHY YOU
WENT AWAY; HOW OUR LOVE WENT
ASTRAY.

WHEN I DIDN'T HEAR YOUR VOICE, I
KNEW YOU MADE THAT CHOICE.
SHOULD I REJOICE?

MAYBE, IN REAL-TIME,
YOU WEREN'T REALLY MINE.
TRUST ME—I'LL BE FINE.
THE LOVE I HAD FOR YOU WAS REAL. I
ENJOYED THE WAY YOU MADE ME FEEL.

NOW, YOU'RE GONE. OK. NO BIG DEAL.

I DIDN'T GET A GOODBYE KISS.
YOU'LL TRULY WILL BE MISSED, BUT
I'LL GET OVER THIS.

WHEN ONE DOOR CLOSES, WE ALWAYS

OPPOSE IT. SOMETIMES, JUST SMELL THE
ROSES.

BETTER DAYS ARE YET TO COME. RELAX, DATE,
AND HAVE SOME FUN. BELIEVE YOU'LL FIND
YOUR CHOSEN ONE.

WHAT IS FAMILY?

ALTHOUGH YOUR BLOOD RUNS THROUGH ME,
WE ARE NOT FAMILY.
OUR ROOTS JUST COME FROM THE SAME TREE;
THAT'S THE ONLY BOND BETWEEN YOU AND ME.
NOT SURE WHAT FAMILY SUPPOSED TO BE.
COEXISTING THROUGH MEMORIES,
I TRY LISTENING TO STORIES ABOUT OUR
ANCESTRY.
STILL NO CONNECTION BETWEEN YOU AND ME.
WE SHARE A RELATED HISTORY.
I GUESS THAT'S WHAT MAKES US FAMILY.

SOULMATE

YOU WERE MY SOULMATE;
I KNEW RIGHT OUT THE GATE.
THE LOVE WE HAD WAS GREAT.
SOME PEOPLE MAY DEBATE.

THOUGHT YOU WERE THE LOVE OF MY LIFE
UNTIL I FOUND OUT ABOUT YOUR WIFE.
NOW, OUR LOVE IS IN STRIFE.
FELT LIKE YOU STABBED ME WITH A KNIFE.

NOW, I MUST START AGAIN.
CAN'T LIVE IN SIN.
WILL I EVER FIND TRUE LOVE AGAIN?
WILL I GIVE UP ON MEN?
IS THIS MY LOVE'S END?

LONELY BUT NOT ALONE

WHILE I SIT AT HOME,
I AM IN MY OWN TIME ZONE.
SOMETIMES, I FEEL LONELY, BUT I'M NEVER
ALONE.

HAD TO FIND WHAT INTERESTED ME.
HAD TO FIND MY INNER PEACE.
FOUND WAYS TO LOVE ME,
WHETHER IT'S MEDITATING, TRAVELING, OR A BRIEF
SHOPPING SPREE—
EVEN SPENDING TIME WITH FAMILY.
THESE ARE THE THINGS THAT COMFORT ME.

WHEN I SIT BY MYSELF,
I DON'T NEED NOBODY ELSE.
I KNOW I HAVE GOD'S GRACE AND GOOD HEALTH.
THAT'S A BLESSING MORE THAN WEALTH.
I'VE LEARNED TO LIVE, LOVE, AND HAVE JOY WITH
MYSELF.

WHEN LIFE HITS

WHEN LIFE HITS,

I SIT DOWN AND JUST WRITE SHIT.

IT HELP RELIEVES STRESS

MY LIFE AND THE WORLD CAN SOMETIMES BE A MESS.

I STARTED WRITING WHEN MY SON DIED.

IT HELPED ME FROM COMMITTING SUICIDE.

THE SADNESS I FELT, THERE WAS NO DENYING.

DIDN'T WANT TO LIVE; COULDN'T STOP CRYING.

 THEY SAY GOD WON'T GIVE YOU MORE THAN YOU CAN HANDLE,

SO I PRAYED AND THEN LIT A CANDLE.

OH, LORD, WHAT IS MY PURPOSE HERE?

I HEARD A LIGHT WHISPER IN MY EAR:

SOME ANGELS ARISE AND RECEIVE THEIR WINGS.

OTHERS STAY HERE AND CREATE BEAUTIFUL THINGS.

THAT'S WHEN I BEGAN WRITING MY STORY;

IT WAS FROM GOD'S GRACE AND HIS GLORY.

MY FIRST WAS A LETTER TO MY SON,

LETTING HIM KNOW HOW I FELT WHEN HIS WORLD BEGUN.

THEN, I SAT DOWN TO WRITE

ABOUT THE WORLD'S PLIGHT

AND HOW WE NEED TO STAND UP FOR OUR HUMAN RIGHTS.

I WROTE ABOUT OUR MELANIN SKIN

AND CAUCASIANS; THEIR ANCESTORS AND THEIR SINS.

WE CAN TAKE A KNEE WHEN WE PRAY,

JUST, LORD, DON'T DO IT ON FOOTBALL DAY.

WE CREATE A LIFETIME OF WONDERFUL MEMORIES

JUST TO STRUGGLE TO REMEMBER ME

THE LIFE I ONCE HAD.

NOT GONNA REMEMBER IF I WAS HAPPY OR SAD.

GRIEF

LIFE IS LIKE A ROLLERCOASTER RIDE,
FILLED WITH EMOTIONS YOU CAN'T
KEEP INSIDE.

ONE MINUTE, YOU ARE AS
HAPPY AS CAN BE. THE NEXT MINUTE, YOU ARE
CRYING ENOUGH TO WATER SEVERAL TREES.

THE MEMORIES OF THE LOVED ONES
WHO HAVE GONE AWAY
IMPACTS OUR LIFE EVERY DAMN DAY.

IT COULD BE THE SCENT OF PERFUME,
A TV SHOW, OR A TRIP TO A MUSEUM.
TEARS WILL START FALLING, WISHING
YOU COULD JUST SEE THEM.

IT DOESN'T MATTER IF IT'S YOUR
MOM, DAD, DAUGHTER, OR SON. IT'S
ALL ABOUT GRIEVING ANY LOVED ONE.

I REMEMBER IN 2001 WHEN MY
STRUGGLES BEGUN.

GRIEF STARTED FOR ME WHEN DEATH
CLAIMED SEVEN MEMBERS OF MY FAMILY.

WITH EVERY PHONE CALL RING,
ANOTHER ANGEL RECEIVED THEIR WINGS.

IT STARTED WITH MY NEPHEW,
MISAEL. THEN, MY COUSIN, MY IN-
LAWS, MY GRANDMA, AND MY AUNT
IDABEL. THAT WEEK WAS A LIVING HELL.

AT THE END OF THE DAY,
IT'S ALWAYS GOD'S WILL HIS WAY

DEMENTIA

What is my name?
Don't be ashamed.
Age has got your mind in another time frame.

Five minutes ago, I was your daughter who you
loved so deeply. Now, I am your mother or sister; it
changes weekly.

I say what is my name
Any minute, it can change.

Your conversations are repetitive,
As you talk to me like I'm just a relative.

On your good days, I see your shine.
On your bad days, you've lost so much time.
You can't get it right in your mind.

You know the name of your grandkids,
But some days, you can't remember having kids.

Again, I say, *What is my name?*
Not to make you feel ashamed;
Just to see your time frame.

STATE OF DEPRESSION

I'M IN A STATE OF DEPRESSION.
I CAN'T MOVE; MY BODY IS IN A RECESSION.
MY MIND AND THOUGHTS ARE IN SUSPENSION.
IT'S SO HARD TO MAKE A SOUND DECISION.

I'M STUCK;
I CAN'T MOVE. I WANT TO GIVE UP.
I DON'T KNOW WHO REALLY GIVES A FUCK.
I JUST PRAY; OH GOD, WISH ME GOOD LUCK.

TRYING TO HEAL.
JUST DON'T KNOW HOW TO FEEL.
SOMETIMES, I JUST CAN'T DEAL. THESE
FEELINGS ARE SO REAL.

GOTTA GET MY MIND RIGHT.
TRYING TO FIND MY GUIDING LIGHT;
IT USED TO SHINE SO BRIGHT.
HOPEFULLY, I'LL BE ALRIGHT.

SLEEPLESS NIGHTS

WHEN I CAN'T SLEEP AT NIGHT,
LAYING DOWN, HOLDING MY PILLOW TIGHT,
PRAYING WITH ALL MY MIGHT
THAT I'LL FALL TO SLEEP BEFORE DAYLIGHT.

I FINALLY CLOSE MY EYES.
MY SLEEP PATTERN HAS BEEN COMPROMISED.
MUCH TO MY SURPRISE,
I CAN ONLY FALL ASLEEP TO THE SUNRISE.

MY MIND IS ALWAYS RACING.
MY THOUGHTS ARE CONSTANTLY RETRACING.
THIS NEW LIFE I'M EMBRACING.
THOSE OLD THOUGHTS I'M ERASING.

MY OLD THOUGHTS ARE TOO MUCH.
I TRY TO REST, BUT NO LUCK.
SLEEPING IS A MUST.
IN GOD I DO TRUST.

I FINALLY FALL ASLEEP,
ONLY TO HEAR THE ALARM GO BEEP.
MY HOUSE IS QUIET; NOT A PEEP.
ANOTHER NIGHT GONE BY. STILL, NO SLEEP.

DREAMS

LIFE IS ABOUT A DREAM.

WHAT DOES THAT REALLY MEAN?

WHAT DO YOU DREAM ABOUT?

HOW CAN YOU MAKE YOUR DREAMS SPROUT?

YOUR DREAMS ARE A DEEP IMAGINATION.

KEEP TRYING TO MAKE IT A REALIZATION.

I'M TRYING MY BEST

TO MAKE MY DREAMS MANIFEST.

WRITING A BOOK OF RHYMES,

DEALING WITH LIFE AND HARD TIMES.

I'M MY LIFE'S EXPRESSIONS:

IT'S HOW I DEAL WITH MY DREAMS, LIFE, AND THE WORLD'S TRANSGRESSIONS

AS I SIT BACK AND DAYDREAM,

I CAN ONLY TELL YOU WHAT MY DREAMS MEAN.

SEASONED PEOPLE

AS I LAY AROUND WATCHING THE SNOW FALL DOWN,

IT AMAZES MY MIND HOW GOD CREATED EACH SNOWFLAKE A DIFFERENT DESIGN.

WE HAVE FOUR SEASONS; THE WEATHER CHANGES FOR DIFFERENT REASONS.

WHEN FALL COMES AROUND, WE WATCH THE BEAUTIFUL LEAVES CHANGE AND FALL DOWN.

WINTER STARTS WITH A COLD BREEZE. THEN, THE TEMPERATURE DROPS UNTIL ITS A FREEZE.

I LOVE THE SPRING. IT'S THE START OF NEW THINGS.

SUMMER BRINGS THE SUN SO BRIGHT. I ENJOY THOSE HOT SUMMER NIGHTS.

THE WEATHER CHANGES WITH DIFFERENT SEASONS; PEOPLE CHANGE FOR DIFFERENT REASONS.

YOU CAN ACCEPT PEOPLE FOR WHO THEY ARE AND STILL LOVE THEM FROM AFAR.

SO, CHOOSE WISELY WHO YOU WILL KEEP. CHOOSE THOSE WHO BRING YOUR HEART INNER PEACE.

I AM THANKFUL FOR FRIENDS WHO ARE NOW FAMILY. I WILL LOVE YOU ENDLESSLY.

SOME PEOPLE ARE HERE FOR ONLY WHAT YOU CAN GIVE. THOSE PEOPLE I PRAY FOR. MOVE ON AND FORGIVE.

EVERYONE YOU MEET ARE FOR DIFFERENT REASONS. SOME ARE HERE FOR LIFE; OTHERS ARE HERE FOR SEASONS.

JEALOUSY

WHY ARE YOU JEALOUS OF ME?

CAN'T HELP IT, WE'RE BUILT DIFFERENTLY.

YOU HAVE TO WORK ON YOUR OWN INFIDELITY.

MY AURA IS OF SUPERIORITY,

BUT MY HEART HAS LOVE AND GENEROSITY.

GRAB AHOLD OF ME;

COME GET ALL THIS POSITIVE ENERGY.

LET'S CLIMB TOGETHER AND STRIVE
SUCCESSFULLY.

POSITIVE VIBES ARE ALL YOU NEED.

STOP HATING AND ACTING RESENTFULLY;

YOU'RE BLOCKING YOUR BLESSINGS. ACTUALLY,

GOD GAVE TALENTS TO BOTH YOU AND ME.

HIS STORY VS OUR HISTORY

WHAT IS BLACK HISTORY?
A RECREATION OF HIS STORY,
NOT THE TRUTH ABOUT OUR GLORY.

WE ARE PEOPLE OF GREAT.
PEOPLE TRIED TO BREAK
OUR STORY, WE MUST RECREATE

THE STRONGEST PEOPLE ARE BLACK;
THIS COUNTRY WAS BUILT ON OUR BACKS.
THIS IS NOT A MYTH, BUT A TRUE FACT.

WE HAD OUR OWN TOWNS.
THEY BURNT IT ALL DOWN.
JUST DIDN'T WANT US AROUND.

IF WE CAN TELL OUR OWN STORY,
IT WOULD TELL OF OUR GREATNESS AND GLORY.
WE WERE NOT ONLY SLAVES; THAT'S JUST HIS
STORY.

WE WERE DOCTORS, LAWYERS, AND BUSINESSMEN,
GREAT PEOPLE FROM WAY BACK WHEN,
TILL THEY INVADED OUR LAND AND KILLED OUR
MEN.

THEY BEAT AND ENSLAVED US.
THEY RAPED OUR WOMEN AND ENGRAVED US.
WE WORKED THEIR FIELDS FROM DAY TO DUST.

A TUNNEL WAS BUILT FOR US TO FOLLOW.
OTHERS DIED FIGHTING FOR OUR FREEDOM, OUR SORROW.
SOME ESCAPED AND BUILT NEW CITIES FOR A BETTER TOMORROW.

SO, LET US NOT ONLY LEARN HIS STORY.
REMEMBER OUR ANCESTORS IN GLORY.
LET US REWRITE OUR OWN HISTORY.

AMERIKKKA'S JUSTICE

AMERIKKKA AT ITS BEST!
FUCK THE LAWS AND OUR UNREST!

THIS COUNTRY WAS BUILT
TO EXPLOIT THE BLACK MAN'S GUILT.

WE SERVE EXTRA TIME,
ALTHOUGH WE COMMIT THE SAME CRIMES.

THEY CLAIM THIS IS THE LAND OF THE FREE,
BUT THEY AIN'T TALKING ABOUT YOU AND ME.

IF YOU'RE WHITE
YOU CAN'T PROTECT BLACK RIGHTS.
THEY'LL KILL YOU, ALL RIGHT?
AND THEY THINK THAT SHIT IS RIGHT.

YOU'LL BE A DISGRACE
GOING AGAINST YOUR OWN RACE.
NOW, YOU'RE CONSIDERED "BLACK FACE."

JUSTICE WILL ONLY PREVAIL
WHEN THEY'RE CONVICTED AND SENT TO JAIL.

WE MAY HAVE TO ARM EVERY BLACK MAN
AND TAKE BACK THIS FORSAKEN LAND.

THIS COUNTRY WAS BUILT ON OUR ANCESTORS'
BACKS.
THIS IS A TRUE HISTORICAL FACT.

I HAVE NO MORE TO SAY.
THIS IS JUSTICE THE AMERIKKKAN WAY.

WHAT IS OUR PLIGHT

What is our plight?

Why do we always have to fight?

What are our God-given rights?

Didn't God give us rights?

You thought these laws were for us all right?

What can we do to make this right?

Learn our Black is a beautiful sight.

We have to stick together; become tight.

Show them we can unite,

From our plight

Of the poor

Showing the nation, we deserve more.

We are not going to endure

The struggles of our ancestors before.

We're tired of marching, trying to even the score.

We have to begin to educate

So we can elevate.

To demonstrate

A plan

So we can become leaders of this land.

Land of the free

For you and me.

GUILT

THIS LAND WAS BUILT
ONLY FOR A BLACK MAN'S GUILT.

WE MARCHED IN PEACE FOR FREEDOM.
THEY MARCHED ALONGSIDE US WITH GUNS,
THINKING, *WE GONNA MAKE THESE NIGGAS RUN.*

WHEN WILL THIS SHIT EVER END?
WE CAN'T EVEN CONVICT THESE RACIST
AMERI**KKK**ANS.

THEY STOLE US FROM OUR LAND
TO MAKE US SLAVES FOR THE WHITE MAN.

WE KNOW HISTORICAL FACTS.
THIS LAND WAS BUILT ON OUR ANCESTORS'
BACKS.

BEEN STOPPED BELIEVING THIS LAND WAS FREE.
THEY KEEP KILLING PEOPLE WHO LOOK LIKE ME.

IF YOU'RE WHITE AND STAND FOR BLACK RIGHTS,
THEY'LL KILL YOU, TOO, AND THINK IT'S ALL RIGHT.

YOU CAN'T GO AGAINST YOUR RACE,
'CAUSE NOW YOU'RE CONSIDERED "**BLACK FACE.**"

JUSTICE CAN ONLY PREVAIL
WHEN WE START SEEING THEM CONVICTED AND
JAILED.

I'M NEVER SURPRISED
AT THE WHITE MAN'S JUSTICE AND THIS
COUNTRY'S DEMISE.

GOD'S CHILDREN

Is this the land of the free?

Is this the home of the brave?

We are not free.

We are still enslaved.

I believed in that dream,

But what does that dream mean?

All our Martin Luther Kings

Are being shot or dying on a string.

You hate us and our skin

Because of your ancestors' sin.

Not sure why we are not equal

When we're all GOD'S people.

When will we be free at last?

Or will our present and future always be our history's past?

WE RISE

~

We tried to kneel.
The slack we got was so unreal.

We marched with Martin Luther King, shouting, Let freedom ring!

We stood with Malcolm X and the nation became vexed.

We're fighting for black lives lost. We're gonna fight no matter the cost.

They burned us down in 1921—that ain't even when this begun.

They stole us from our land. They raped us and killed us, man!

In 1955, they beat Emmett till he died. We've lost so many lives. Our revolution is how we'll rise.

WHAT IS IT ABOUT OUR SKIN

What is it about our skin

That makes you hate us within? Is it really just our beautiful melanin, or guilt **from your ancestors' sin?**

Thought once **Barack became President** that you could accept and respect our presence.

We walked with pride with our heads held high. Now, hands held high,

Trying to reach for the sky, knowing no matter what, we gonna die, whether we resist or comply. **How do we keep our race alive?**

We are preachers and teachers; lawyers and politicians. Although we're qualified and hold the same positions, we are proud people, still fighting to be equal.

Stop judging us by the color of our skin. Get to know us and love us from within. We don't judge you for your ancestors' sin. We are all GOD'S CHILDREN.

THIS IS WHY WE KNEEL

Our melanin is our sin.

They'll never love our Black skin.

They'll call cops on us

So they can slay us.

These injustices they use to enslave us.

We can't take a stand.

This really *ain't* our land.

When we take a knee

In this country, we *ain't* free.

These laws not made for you and me.

We must face reality.

Until we Lose that slave mentality,

His Story

Will always be Our Story.

His History

Will be our Misery.

BIDEN AND HARRIS

All Americans can rejoice!

We voted and used our voice.

Biden and Harris were our choices.

We got rid of President 45;

so tired and weary from his lies.

This country barely survived

Corona taking many American lives.

We'll begin to try and heal from this

with our new President number 46.

This presidential victory

will go down in history.

Kamala is our new VP,

and she looks like you and me— another notch in
our Black History.

COVID

THOUGHT THE SPRING WAS GONNA BE LIT.
I PLANNED AND BOOKED SEVERAL TRIPS,
THEN COVID HIT.

THE CITY WAS SHUT DOWN.
NOBODY COULD MOVE AROUND;
EVERYTHING CLOSED IN THIS TOWN.

PEOPLE BEGAN DYING.
FAMILIES ARE CRYING.
THE WORLD WAS SHOOK; THERE'S NO DENYING.

TRYING TO SALVAGE THIS POPULATION
FROM THIS DISEASE AND DEVASTATION
THAT RAN RAMPANT ACROSS ALL THE NATION.

MASK UP! PLEASE, TAKE NO RISKS.
THIS COVID SHIT STILL EXISTS.
THIS AIN'T A HISTORICAL MYTH.

I STAYED HOME AND RELAXED
UNTIL THEY CAME UP WITH THIS VAX.
COLLECTED UNEMPLOYMENT TO THE MAX.

NOW, THERE'S A MANDATE.
EVERYONE MUST VACCINATE.

DON'T PROCRASTINATE.

SOME PEOPLE WANT TO DEBATE,
WORRIED ABOUT THAT SYPHILIS TREATMENT WE
WERE FORCED TO PARTICIPATE.
I CAN RELATE.

DON'T LET HISTORY DICTATE
DO YOUR RESEARCH, INVESTIGATE,
CHOOSE WISELY. IT'S YOUR OWN FATE.

I PRAY EVERY DAY
THAT COVID WILL GO AWAY AND THIS IS NOT OUR
DOOMSDAY.

About the Author

Good day, my book buyers and readers!

My name is Monica Thompson. I was born on March 31, 1961, and raised by my mother, Marguerite Horsey-Goodwin.

My mother was married three times, which led me to have one biological brother, Montague Thompson III (now deceased), four bonus sisters, and two bonus brothers.

I am an honors college graduate and I've earned a Bachelor of Science degree in business administration. I have held several, jobs but my last employment of twenty-three years was with the NYC transit authority. Retired from NYC transit seven years ago, and I am now part-owner of a catering business called Corb the Chef Inc.

I'm a mother of three beautiful children. My son, Claudio Gene Lake,

Jr. (aka Maddox Madison) was born on April 7, 1986 and passed away on June 19, 2014. My daughter, Ashleigh Domonique Lake (aka Amazin), was born on May 3, 1990. I have another daughter/niece named Sharmane Vazquez, who I adopted. She was born on May 18,1981 and I adopted her on October 31,1994.

Growing up in Harlem, New York, I lived comfortably in a three-bedroom apartment with my children and my nieces. My niece, Starr Monique Thompson, was born on July 4, 1981.

After the loss of my son, I began writing down my feelings and my expressions. I had a very difficult time coping with this loss and needed a way to express and release my emotions.

I hope everyone enjoyed reading *Reflections of Life's Journey*

Reflection Photos

(Claudio, Ashleigh, and Monica)

(Ashleigh Domonique Lake aka AMAZIN)

Claudio, Ashleigh & Me

Marguerite (my mom) and me

Me and my Daughters (Sharmane and Ashleigh)

Magnificent 7 left to right (Gus, Sharon, Edri, Barry, Me, Sophia & Darryl)

The Graysons (Sharnee, Dee, Dj, RayJon & Princess DasJa)

("The Thompson Clan")

My Brothers (Barry & Me, Top Right Montague aka Que, bottom right Darryl)

My Sister Friend - Stephanie Brown

My Sister in Love Edri

Jamelah "Sunflower" Kearse

Lightning Source UK Ltd.
Milton Keynes UK
UKHW052110250722
406371UK00001B/3